MICHAE

A Life From Beginning to End

Copyright © 2017 by Hourly History.

Table of Contents

Introduction

Michael Faraday was the son of a North Yorkshire-born blacksmith. Faraday grew up in poor surroundings in west London and received only the most perfunctory education. But he possessed an enquiring mind—one which needed to understand the way the world worked. This drove Faraday to experiment and test his theories constantly.

He educated himself through reading to such a degree that he was able to secure employment in the vaunted Royal Institution, hired by one of the foremost men of science of the age. Once there, Faraday would rise to become one of the most famous scientists in history, his opinions sought by governments all over the world. He would achieve this fame despite his lowly origins and in a society that did not easily accept progression through the social hierarchy. This would have been made even more difficult by his devotion to a dissenter church which rejected the Anglican establishment along with all of its institutions.

Faraday's discoveries in the field of electricity and magnetism would open new theoretical fields of study and new avenues of technology that would transform human society across the globe.

This book will tell the story of the life of Michael Faraday. It will cover the discoveries he made and the inventions those discoveries made possible and highlight how our modern society has been shaped by his work.

But, it is first necessary to tell the story of his parents. Their decision to move to London would mean that their third child, Michael, would be born in a city of great opportunity for an enquiring mind.

Chapter One

The Apprentice

"I learned at that time some of my philosophy and set various things beside iron saucepans & pots afloat - for jugs bottles & many other things that I thought at first ought to sink floated & so many first steps to knowledge were gained."

—Michael Faraday in a letter recalling his boyhood

James Faraday came from a family that had achieved some modest business success in North Yorkshire. His brother, Richard, owned two houses and two mills in the town of Kirkby Stephen. James left the town to take up the profession of blacksmith in the village of Outhgill, about five miles to the south. He married Margaret Hastwell on June 11, 1786. Circumstances soon forced the family to relocate. The area in which Outhgill lay, the Eden Valley of what was then known as Westmorland, was rural and sparsely populated. James' business relied on supplying shoes to the horses of coaches passing through. And in 1788 a drought meant a shortage of hay and a subsequent fall in the number of travelers using Outhgill as a rest stop for their horses.

Subsequently, James and Margaret took their family to London. This decision was to mean that Michael Faraday would be born, and grow up, in the capital. It would have a pivotal effect on his life. The decision to move was not just an economic one. There also appears to have been a strong, spiritual motivation for James and Margaret which would have a profound effect on Michael Faraday. James was a member of the Sandemanian church. This church was founded in London by Robert Sandeman as a separate faith from the Anglican church. In fact, the Sandemanians were a splinter of a splinter, forming as a result of a schism in the Inghamite church established in Yorkshire by Bernard Ingham in the 1740s. James' father had been a member of that church and had subsequently moved to the Sandemanian faith.

James Faraday's employer in London was a member of the Sandemanian church, which counted a number of families among its congregation. It may have been the joint lure of employment and spiritual community that made James' decision to move to London. After all, this which would have been a significant distance to travel for a relatively poor family from the far north-west of England. For James Faraday's son, religion would be an important factor throughout his life. And his parents' decision to relocate allowed Michael to grow up surrounded by the industry, invention, and ideas of one of the world's foremost cities as well as giving him the spiritual scaffolding that would become an integral part of his character.

Michael Faraday was born on September 22, 1791, in Newington Butts, Southwark, a mile from Blackfriars Bridge. He was the third Faraday child, after Elizabeth and Robert. The family moved before Michael was five to Jacob's Mews, near Manchester Square in west London. His older siblings had been baptized into the Anglican church. But by the time of Michael's birth, James Faraday had made his Confession of Faith (a requirement of becoming a full-fledged member of the Sandemanian church), and both Michael and his younger sister Margaret (born when Michael was 11) were baptized into the Sandemanian church.

Jacob's Mews was to be Michael Faraday's childhood home with his parents remaining there until he was 18 years old. Michael attended school to learn the three Rs—reading, 'riting, and 'rithmetic. While this took care of the most basic rudiments of education, Michael was inclined even as a child to learn from observation and experimentation. This was to be a major facet of his career in science. When a canal was built near his home and he saw the first coal barges traveling on it, it inspired him to try out various materials to see if they would float or sink. London at that time was expanding, but it was also significantly smaller than today. Michael lived on the outskirts of the city and so could see the technological developments that went with the urban expansion, as well as the natural world.

On September 22, 1804, his 13th birthday, Faraday was given employment as an errand boy to George Ribeau, a bookseller, binder, and publisher. Faraday worked for Ribeau for a year before being formally apprenticed to him on October 7, 1805. During this time, Michael left the family home to move in with his new master at 2 Blandford Street. The apprenticeship was to last seven years and would not only teach Faraday the trade of bookbinding, as he took up the practice of reading, after hours, the books he was being taught to bind. In 1809, at the age of 18, Faraday was maintaining a *Philosophical Miscellany* which included scientific entries copied from such sources as the *Encyclopedia Britannica*. In these studies, Faraday would come across two books in particular that would shape his later life as a scientist.

The first was *The Improvement of the Mind* by Isaac Watts. This book taught Faraday certain techniques which could be used in the gaining of knowledge, such as maintaining a notebook of experiments and thoughts (a habit Faraday would assiduously follow and which gave later generations valuable insights into his thoughts and theories). The other book was *Conversations in Chemistry* by Jane Marcet. It was from Marcet that Faraday would learn some fundamentals of chemistry. Faraday trusted in verifiable facts and challenged anything else. He found that Marcet's assertions were verifiable through his own experiments, and her work became his anchor in the field.

These two authors can be seen to have influenced Faraday into the adoption of the scientific method—namely thoroughly documenting experiments and the pursuit of verifiable truth. The emergence of the famous man of science can be seen in the enthusiasm of the young Faraday for these works.

In 1810, Faraday discovered a series of lectures being delivered by a John Tatum at his home of 53 Dorset Street. There was an admission price of one shilling which

Faraday was given by his brother, who was following in their father's trade as a blacksmith. This would be the young Faraday's first exposure to a scientific lecture. Previously his learning had all been in books followed by his own experiments to verify what he was reading. He met other keen students at Tatum's lectures who would remain lifelong friends, including Benjamin Abbott. He would correspond with Abbott frequently and throughout his life. This correspondence and Abbott's recollections all serve to illustrate Faraday's early character and direction. Abbott recalled Faraday conducting his experiments in the kitchen of Jacob's Mews and his first lectures from the end of that table.

Faraday was clearly of a sharp and questing mind from a young age. This is demonstrated by his pursuance of his education, whether by reading the books he was binding or attending lectures.

Chapter Two

From Bookbinder to Man of Science

"I could trust a fact but always cross-examined an assertion."

—Michael Faraday

Faraday's apprenticeship ended on October 6, 1812, and instead, he entered into the role of a journeyman for Henri De La Roche at 5 King Street. Faraday's father, James, had died in 1810 and he decided to move in with his widowed mother.

Now Michael's interest in science was beginning to overshadow his interest in his chosen profession. At this time, he was attending the lectures of John Tatum. Faraday's diaries record 13 such attendances between February 1810 and September 1811. Half of these lectures were on subjects relating to electricity.

In 1812, George Ribeau shared some of Faraday's notebooks with a customer, William Dance, who was the son of a proprietor of the Royal Institution. Dance was impressed by the mind presented to him on those pages and made Faraday a present of tickets to four lectures by Sir Humphry Davy, Professor of Chemistry at the Royal

Institution. Thus Faraday had, through good fortune and diligent note-taking, been steered into the orbit of a man of science who would be a strong influence on his burgeoning scientific career.

Faraday attended the Davy lectures from March to April 1812. He is described as making copious notes as Davy lectured on the definition of acidity. Davy made demonstrations to debunk the accepted view that acids all contained oxygen by producing the compound hydrochloric acid, which contained no oxygen. Faraday was well used to attending scientific lectures and no stranger to the field of chemistry. But what was most significant to the 20-year-old was the experiments. Faraday had long found a need to verify the opinions and theories of those scientists he had been reading about while apprenticed to George Ribeau and employed by Henri De La Roche. It was a fundamental part of his character. In Davy's lectures, he saw a prominent scientific man disproving accepted theory through practical experimentation and demonstration.

Faraday must have been inspired by seeing the Davy lectures. He had expressed to friends his dissatisfaction with his profession as a bookbinder, and his desire to find scientific employment. In one letter Faraday makes reference to a potential job which required him to have knowledge of mathematics and mechanics, which he did not have. He also wrote to Joseph Banks in 1812, seeking employment of a scientific nature and requesting any position no matter how menial. Faraday's stated, however, that he received no answer.

There is some hopelessness evident in Faraday's letters of this period regarding his prospects for employment. But things were about to change. He was advised by his former master, Georges Ribeau, to write to Humphry Davy after Faraday had indicated that he would like to meet the great man. Ribeau encouraged Faraday to send his notebooks which contained his extensive lecture notes. Faraday followed his advice in December 1812. He asked for scientific employment and received an immediate response from Davy inviting him for a meeting in January. Davy subsequently employed Faraday as an amanuensis, after Davy had injured his eyes in a chemical explosion. And in March 1813, Faraday was given the vacant post of laboratory assistant in the Royal Institute, including accommodation within the Institute itself.

Chapter Three

The Royal Institution

"Science is a harsh mistress."

—Sir Humphry Davy

The Royal Institute was founded in 1799 at a meeting held at the home of the President of the Royal Society, Joseph Banks. The Royal Institution was intended to be for the sharing of knowledge and the application of that knowledge in general life. The Institute was to prove the perfect launching pad for Faraday's scientific career and the securing of a post within the Royal Institution must, to Faraday, have seemed the realization of a dream. Faraday had completed the transition from the trade of bookbinding to the world of science. Initially, he appears to have been primarily employed as an assistant to Sir Humphry Davy. Amongst other enterprises, he continued the experiments with nitrogen trichloride which had damaged Davy's eyes and given Faraday his first opportunity. In 1815, Faraday was acknowledged by Davy for his assistance in the development of the miner's safety lamp—the so-called Davy lamp.

Faraday's humble origins meant that despite his intellect and ability he was not looked upon as being a gentleman and therefore was not of the same social level as Davy and others within the Institution. In 1813, Davy invited Faraday to accompany him and his wife on a tour of Europe. The tour would be cut short, however, by the resumption of the war with France, following Napoleon's escape from exile on the island of Elba. Faraday was to act as Davy's scientific assistant on this trip and also as his valet. Though Faraday's employment was with the Royal Institution and not Davy personally, Davy was the most senior and respected scientist of his age. His influence was considerable and had worked in Faraday's favor in allowing him to take up the chance to work at the Royal Institution. But his lowly birth and Davy's elevated rank meant that Faraday would find himself being exploited, to a degree, by his initially more illustrious senior.

On June 12, 1821, Faraday got married to Sarah Barnard. Sarah was a member of the same church as Faraday, the Sandemanians. The two would never have children, but Faraday's letters display his devotion to his wife until his death. Sarah Faraday would become his rock, organizing the household.

By this time Faraday was establishing a reputation as a chemist in his own right. In 1821, he was asked by an old friend to review the published work on electromagnetism by Danish scientist Hans Oersted. In order to gain an understanding of the work, Faraday repeated Oersted's experiments. As the young boy had done to learn which materials would float or sink, Faraday still learned by experimentation. By September 4, 1821, he discovered that a wire carrying electrical current could be made to move around a magnet. Faraday described this phenomenon as electromagnetic rotations. It is the principle behind the electric motor. This work and others would lead to Faraday being elected a Fellow of the Royal Society on January 8, 1824, at the age of 32.

Despite his fellowship, Faraday would find himself still filling the role of pseudo-assistant to Sir Humphry Davy. In the tasks he was given, it is clear that his talent was being exploited by Davy, as Faraday gained little by the completion of the tasks, all of which Davy had been charged with completing. Three main demands emerged on Faraday's time during the 1820s. The first of these was the founding of a sister organization to sit alongside the Royal Society and contain the Royal Society's non-scientific members. The purpose of this society would be to ensure that the Royal Society remained the home of men of science only. A meeting of interested parties was held on February 16, 1824, to establish a club, which would simply be called the Society. Faraday was made the club's first secretary. Through February and March 1824, Faraday had to send out hundreds of letters to various scientists, artists, writers, and clergymen to join the new society. The club was renamed the Athenaeum in February 1824.

Faraday was offered £100 per annum to keep the position of secretary which he initially refused, suggesting a friend of his, Edward Magrath. When Magrath was unable to take up his position, Faraday took up the job until May 1824. In recognition, Faraday was given a year's subscription for free. The Athenaeum Club still exists and has been very successful as a society for intellectuals, with

52 Nobel prize winners among its members. However, Faraday seems to have found it to be a waste of his time and subsequently resigned.

The second onerous task to which Faraday was forced was the project to prevent saltwater corrosion of the copper bottoms of Royal Navy ships. This task would occupy both Davy and Faraday—in particular the latter—from 1824 to 1826. Faraday's tasks in this project were to undertake experimental testing to understand the problem and allow Davy to come up with a solution. Michael was then supposed to conduct further experiments to see if the proposed solution worked. Davy concluded that an electrical reaction between the copper and the seawater occurred which caused copper salts to form and corrosion to occur. He reasoned that if the electrical polarity between the copper and seawater were reversed this would solve the problem. Davy had already proved that zinc would be the best material to add to the copper to achieve this.

As a result, from mid-February 1824, Faraday began a series of tests on ships moored in Portsmouth Shipyard. In April all Royal Navy vessels were fitted with a zinc protector, and the state of the hull was monitored over a period of months to observe the effect. The experiment failed, as the lack of chemical reaction meant that the toxic copper salts were no longer present and ships were reporting significant amounts of barnacle and seaweed on their hulls. Blame for the failure was passed from the Admiralty to Davy. He subsequently began to suffer ill health and would resign his position as President of the

Royal Society on November 6, 1827. This would be an important development for Faraday as it would eliminate the major barrier to his fully pursuing his own experiments, and this could all be achieved without having to leave the Royal Institution.

The third task undertaken began in 1824 when Davy was still being lauded for his ship protectors. The task consisted of producing a high-quality optical glass. A joint committee of the Board of Longitude and the Royal Society was formed in 1824 to produce better glass, which could be used to improve navigational instruments. The committee appointed a glass making firm and approached Faraday to analyze the glass produced. This work went on until the failure of Davy's protectors and Davy's subsequent resignation from the committee. When the committee next met, Faraday was tasked with manufacturing his own glass, as the glass produced by others had failed to meet expectations.

Faraday's task was to produce the high-quality optical glass through introducing a heavy metal such as lead to the molten glass. The problem with the process was that the metal would sink to the bottom; stirring would take care of this issue but that act, in turn, would produce bubbles which would distort the glass. This had been proven by an Austrian optician named Joseph Fraunhofer. Faraday's job was to replicate Fraunhofer's experiments. He began this task in December 1827, and it would take up most of this time.

Faraday was becoming frustrated with the loss of his time in these experiments. But he could hardly prevent his exploitation by Davy, given the social gap between them. Faraday had successfully made the transition from skilled tradesman to a respected experimentalist. But the time-consuming work to which he was being put was preventing him from his areas of interest. Faraday was thinking of ways to ensure his financial independence, allowing him greater freedom to choose how to occupy his time. He was appointed Professor of Chemistry at the Royal Military Academy, Woolwich to that end. His desire for independence was further helped by the death, in May 1829, of Sir Humphry Davy. Now, Faraday was free to pursue the ideas which until now he had only been able to make passing reference to in his notebook. These were, in his own words, to "convert magnetism into electricity."

Despite the loss of his time on Davy's experiments, the period that Faraday spent as an assistant to Davy was invaluable. This period allowed Faraday to establish himself within the Royal Society as an experimentalist with specialist knowledge in the field of chemistry. There can be little doubt that without this he wouldn't have been able to secure a professorship, which in turn gave him the financial independence to be able to pursue the experiments that interested him. It's also important to consider his humble origins. This was a society of rigid social hierarchies. Upward mobility in socioeconomic terms did not exist in nineteenth-century England. Faraday was the son of a blacksmith. His family was not wealthy and he, himself, had a background in the trades. It is important not to underestimate the prejudice which would have been held by men such as Sir Humphry Davy for those from the lower classes.

For Faraday to overcome the prejudices of the upper and upper middle classes who populated the halls of the Royal Society would have taken incontrovertible evidence of his intellect and ability. His notebooks would have demonstrated sufficiently that this was a well-read and highly intelligent man. Faraday's almost religious documenting of his thoughts and experiments was the stepping stone that allowed him to move from the obscurity of a journeyman bookbinder to the heights of the Royal Society. Once there, his ability spoke for itself.

Chapter Four

Electricity

"As an answer to those who are in the habit of saying to every new fact, 'What is its use?' . . . The answer of the experimentalist would be, 'Endeavour to make it useful.'"

—Michael Faraday

Faraday managed to use some of his time for his research into electromagnetism in the 1820s. This had to be juggled with other responsibilities. He had been assisting with the delivery of lectures since 1816, but from December 7, 1824, he began a course of 19 lectures on the subject of metals. Then on February 7, 1825, he was appointed Director of the Laboratory and relieved of the onerous responsibility for assisting in lectures. This seems to have allowed him enough free time to pursue his experiments.

He published an article in July 1825 on electromagnetic current in which he showed that current passing through a wire was not affected by magnetism. Later in 1825, he pursued two experiments which were not published but which served to further his understanding and laid the groundwork for later success. In the first, which he entitled "Electromagnetic Induction" he tried and failed to produce electricity in one wire by proximity

A discovery may have no use initially, but it is up to the experimenter to discover its use.

to another which was carrying current. In his second experiment, he spun a copper plate beneath an electroscope (an instrument for detecting and measuring electricity) but failed to detect any electricity in the copper plate. This experiment was inspired by the finding that a spinning copper plate could deflect the needle of a compas, and therefore possessed a magnetic field. Faraday was interested in the link between magnetism and electricity as well as the concept of induction (the influence of electricity across space).

Faraday continued to look for ways to ensure his financial independence, ever mindful of the precariousness of his position at the Royal Society under Davy. He accepted the role of Assistant Superintendent of the House, making him responsible for the upkeep of the buildings of the Royal Institution. While this was an extra burden on his time, it also served to secure his position, making him rather indispensable and thus further insulating him from the demands of Humphry Davy. It was during this time that Faraday instituted two new series of lectures which he hoped would address financial problems the Institution had been facing.

These were the Friday Evening Discourses and the Christmas Lectures for Juveniles. The Christmas lectures in particular became very popular. Faraday was approached by several publishers to commit these lectures to print. This was something he resisted because of the number of experimental demonstrations which made up the talks. Faraday couldn't think of an effective way to include these in a print form. He would eventually relent, but for now, the only way to enjoy Faraday's Christmas Lectures was to attend in person.

The Friday Evening Discourses were exclusive to Institution members, but Faraday appears to have understood the value of these lectures as a means of raising public awareness and support for the Institution. While he was, at first, reluctant to see his lectures formally published, he had no issue with them being covered by journalists. He knew the editors of influential science journals well. One such was William Jerdan of the *Literary Gazette* whom Faraday provided with reports of the Friday lectures for his publication. Faraday took care to invite many other editors of newspapers and journals to ensure press attention. His efforts were rewarded. Membership of the Institution increased significantly through the late 1820s and 1830s.

In 1829, as well as accepting the post of Professor of Chemistry at Woolwich, he also became a founding member of the Admiralty's Resident Scientific Committee. This had been established to replace the Board of Longitude as the provider of state funds for scientific research. The move had been prompted by the failure of Davy to solve the problem of copper corrosion and better optical glass. Though Faraday carried out much experimental work on these projects, no blame appears to have been attached to him. Soon he was the only member and therefore the de facto scientific advisor to the British government. This role would cover a multitude of problems, all of which Faraday appears to have tackled with enthusiasm. His projects included investigating contamination of oatmeal used on prison transport ships, treatment of dry rot, and the use of lightning rods on ships.

So, 1829 was the year in which Faraday must have felt a degree of security. His name was now elevated in establishment circles as an expert, particularly in chemistry, whose advice could be relied upon.

Following Davy's death in May 1829 and Faraday's abandoning of the glass experiment given to him by Davy, Faraday was able to return to induction experiments in earnest in 1831. His experiments "On the production of Electricity from Magnetism" were recorded in his notebook on August 29, 1831. He set up an iron ring with two separate coils of wire wound on opposite sides. When he passed an electrical current through one coil, another current was detected in the second coil. There was no physical connection between them other than the magnetic field of the iron ring.

Faraday had succeeded in observing electromagnetic induction. The apparatus he had used was, in effect, the first electrical transformer (a device for transferring electrical current from one circuit to another through a magnetic field, without physical linkages in between). Transformers are essential to our modern society, used in many applications, not least of which is the transmission of electrical power through a national grid to homes. Faraday was not setting out to invent the transformer. He was an experimentalist, and this was an accidental by-product of his experiments.

He repeated his experiment on the next day with the same results. By October 17, he had discovered how to generate an electrical current by moving a magnet in and out of a coil of wire. On October 28, he worked with a variety of magnets and produced an electrical generator by the rotation of a copper disc between two magnets. The disc was not physically connected to the magnets but produced electricity through induction. Faraday completed his paper, *Experimental Researches into Electricity* by November 22, 1831. The importance of this discovery cannot be overstated as it underpins several pieces of technology which our modern society relies upon. It also opened new avenues of scientific understanding of electricity and magnetism.

After establishing that magnetism could induce an electrical current, Faraday turned his attention to the different forms of electrical power for his next experiments. He wanted to prove that electricity generated by magnetic induction was identical to those arising from other forms, such as static and lightning. Faraday collated all known sources of electrical power as well as experimented to derive new ones. He presented his findings to the Royal Society on December 15, 1832. In the process of seeking to observe all possible sources of electricity, Faraday's experiments took him, for the first time, into the field of electrochemistry. He had assisted Davy in this field many times but had never undertaken his own experiments.

As he began to experiment, he found flaws in the theories which had been held by Davy and others to that point. This was the so-called fluid theory of electricity which Faraday was beginning to refute. With each new experiment into the nature of electrical charge and discharge, he moved his understanding further away from the established theories. By 1833 even the established vocabulary relating to electricity had to be rethought. An entirely new language was needed. Faraday invited William Whewell to come up with new words with which Faraday could describe the world he was uncovering. The words which Whewell conceived included cathode, anode, and ion. All have since entered into common scientific usage.

It is a demonstration of how seriously Faraday took his religion that he found time to take on the role of deacon in his church, even when he was engaged in so much experimental work and scientific publishing. The deacons of the Sandemanian church filled a role of pastoral care, such caring for the sick. Faraday became deacon in 1832, at the same time taking on the responsibility of supporting several orphanages. Faraday's position as a dissenter to the Anglican church could have been another barrier to his advancement. But luckily, such was the success he was achieving with his experiments into electromagnetism that in 1832 Oxford University offered an honorary doctorate to Faraday and three other dissenters. Before this, neither Oxford or Cambridge universities had admitted any non-Anglicans to their institutions.

In October 1834, Faraday published the tenth volume of *Experimental Researches* of which his work on induction had been the first. Following this, he took a three-year hiatus of publication while he sought to clarify his thoughts about the nature of electrical force itself.

In December 1835 he constructed a 12-foot, timber-framed box in the lecture theatre of the Royal Society. It was covered in wire and insulated from the ground by glass supports. Faraday discovered that while the box was charged, he was insulated from that charge if he was inside. Today an apparatus like this would be called a Faraday Cage. The effect which Faraday was seeing was that the external electrical field caused the electrical charges within the cage's conductive material (in Faraday's case the wire covering the box's exterior) to be distributed in such a way that it canceled out the field's effect inside. Today such devices are used today to protect equipment such as radio transmitters or power plants.

For Faraday, this discovery confirmed that electricity was not a fluid but a force. It is another example of Faraday discovering by experimenting. He didn't know that he would end up creating something useful, merely that he wished to map out the lines of the electrical force. The box made of wire and paper was merely the means to achieve this, but the results went beyond his expectations. It proved his theories and validated the direction he had set for himself in his work. To those observing the first Faraday Cage, it would have seemed a machine of wonderful novelty. In Faraday's own words though, the skill of an experimentalist is to "make it useful." Faraday's discovery of electromagnetic rotation would be made useful as the foundation principle of electric motors; his observation of electromagnetic induction would be made useful as the founding principle of the transformer; his attempts to map the lines of electrical force would be made useful in the invention of the Faraday Cage.

In 1836, the Professor of Experimental Philosophy at King's College, Charles Wheatstone was conducting experiments that Faraday found interesting and would go on to repeat. Wheatstone was attempting to measure the velocity of electricity. Faraday would spend 1836 and 1837 repeating Wheatstone's experiments and concluded that a relationship existed between matter, electricity, and light. Wheatstone had been passing a current through half a mile of wire with gaps in the middle and the ends. He observed that the middle spark occurred later than those at the endpoints. Faraday agreed and went further. He used a variety of materials to replace parts of the wires (such as glass or water) and found that where the material was a poor conductor, the middle spark was delayed further. On November 16, 1837, he published his 11th volume of experiments.

In this work he put forward another new word: dielectric, again supplied to him by William Whewell, to describe the electrical state of a non-conducting body between two conductors. The principle of a dielectric is essential in the development of capacitors, which are crucial components of modern electrical circuitry. Faraday also established that induction is the action of contiguous particles which he later defined as particles which were in close proximity to each other. This was an important first step to solving the problem of electrical force acting at a distance or across space. This would form part of his ongoing experiments in the years ahead.

Faraday's observations and theories established in the 1830s have shaken the world. His papers demonstrated principles that have since shaped our modern science and technology. It was Faraday's work in this decade, as well as his performances in the Friday Night Discourses and Christmas Lectures for Juveniles was making him a famous name beyond the scientific community. The press was attending the closed Friday Night Discourses and reported what they saw to the wider public.

In 1835, Prime Minister Robert Peel offered Faraday a pension from the Civil List. He died, however, before the pension could be authorized and his successor, Lord Melbourne took up the offer. But in a meeting with Faraday at Downing Street in October 1835, Melbourne is said to have used profane language to show his contempt for the concept of pensions. Faraday was a deeply religious man and walked out, demanding a written apology. Eventually, this was extracted from the prime minister by the intervention of the king but not before the press discovered the controversy. The incident served to increase Michael Faraday's fame and cement his position as a household name.

There can be no doubt that the development of the twentieth century would have been radically different had it not been for Faraday's discoveries. At the very least, it is clear, that without the knowledge of dielectric materials, transformers and electromagnetic induction, all of which began with Faraday, the pace of technological development in the twentieth century would have been significantly slower.

Chapter Five

Magnetism

"Wonderful as are the laws and phenomenon of electricity when made evident to us in inorganic or dead matter, their interest can bear scarcely any comparison with that which attaches to the same force when connected with the nervous systems and with life."

—Michael Faraday

Faraday was not simply interested in understanding electricity in isolation, nor in the development of technical devices from his theories. He sought an understanding of electricity as part of an overarching theory of all the phenomenon of nature. He mapped out the lines of electrical force exhibited by the gymnotus fish, which used electricity to shock and stun its prey. On November 9, 1838, he published his 15th series of experiments and demonstrated that the electricity generated by the gymnotus fish produced the same effects as electricity generated from other sources.

In the 1840s Faraday had many other demands on his time that appears to have taken him away from his experimental research. He had been appointed scientific advisor to Trinity House in February 1834. Trinity House was the organization set up to have sole responsibility for all lighthouses in England and Wales. By 1841 Faraday was tasked with finding a way to ventilate the light of lighthouses. He developed a double chimney which allowed the by-product of fuel such as oil to be funneled away without clouding the glass and therefore dimming the light. Faraday gave the invention to his brother Robert who worked as a gaslighting contractor. Robert patented the device. This would be the only patented invention from Michael Faraday. His discoveries were not, on the whole, of devices of technology but of theories and principles that described the world.

In the 1840s Faraday's mind turned to magnetism. He formulated the belief that all materials, of any kind, possessed magnetism of some sort. He theorized that the variable which separated materials was temperature. It was known, for example, that metal lost its magnetic field when heated. Cooling it significantly then should produce magnetism, Faraday postulated. He set about attempting to prove this hypothesis in May 1844 by producing extremely low temperatures using a high-pressure pump and then trying to obtain magnetic effects from a wide range of materials.

He failed to find any magnetic effects in materials other than those already known to possess them: nickel, cobalt, and iron. But Faraday was undeterred. Despite the evidence of his experiments, he continued to believe in a universal magnetism and included this in the paper he published showing his findings in January 1845.

On June 24 and 25, 1845, Faraday attended the British Association's Annual Meeting in Cambridge. There he met William Thomson who would become a lifelong friend. It was Thomson who posed the question to Faraday in August 1845 about the effect of a transparent dielectric material on polarized light. Faraday had the opportunity to investigate this question when at the end of August he was asked by Trinity House to test four new lighthouse lamps.

He used a piece of lead glass manufactured during his seemingly fruitless optical glass experiments for Sir Humphry Davy. On September 13, 1845, he proved that the polarization of the light shining through the glass was changed by the magnetic field of a powerful electromagnet. The conclusion to be drawn was that light was affected by electromagnetism. Another new word was coined: magnetics. Materials that were found to be diamagnetic would appear to be non-magnetic to a layman, such as wood or glass. Faraday found that diamagnetic materials were susceptible to magnetic force, they repelled them. Faraday's experiment to prove this was to expose a piece of his heavy glass to a homemade and very powerful electromagnet. The glass aligned itself with the poles of the magnet. Many other experiments have been performed to demonstrate diamagnetism since.

Faraday introduced the world to another new term in his 20th and 21st series of papers, which covered diamagnetism, at the end of 1845: magnetic field. Faraday had succeeded in proving that magnetism was a universal property of all matter. Though he had shown that all matter possesses magnetic properties, he hadn't proved the same about gases. It wasn't until 1847 that he began to look at this problem. Then, the Professor of Experimental Physics at Genoa University, Michele Bancalari, carried out an experiment in which he demonstrated that a flame could be influenced by magnetism. Faraday repeated the experiment on October 23, 1847, and proved that carbon dioxide could be influenced by magnetism. Throughout November 1847 he worked on a variety of gases and was able to confirm that all of them possess magnetic properties.

He returned to this in 1850 with experiments to affect quantities of gas with electromagnets. First, he used a strong container but found there was no effect. Then he tried injecting quantities of gas into soap bubbles and thin, glass test tubes. His experiments confirmed that oxygen in particular had strong magnetic properties. Other gases were found to be diamagnetic. Faraday was not a scientist to seek the expansion of knowledge simply for its own sake. Each successful experiment he undertook was not an end in itself, but more a verification of a theory which would lead him on to a wider theory.

His work on the magnetism of gases is a demonstration of this. Faraday was not content merely to observe a new fact, previously unknown, and so expand the knowledge base of humankind. He wished to apply what he had learned to the whole world. Faraday had taken the ideas of electromagnetism on to the concept of universal magnetism. Now he would take the magnetism of gases and apply it to a theory equally as wide: atmospheric magnetism.

Chapter Six

Quantitative over Qualitative

"The electrical field theory of Faraday and Maxwell represents probably the most profound transformation which has been experienced by the foundations of physics since Newton's time."

—Albert Einstein

Faraday first wrote the words "atmospheric magnetism" in his notebook on July 23, 1850. He would devote himself to this for the next six months. He reasoned that as the magnetism of oxygen lessened when the temperature of the gas lessened, this might be the cause of the so-called magnetic variation phenomenon. This was the phenomenon that caused a variation in the direction of magnetic north and true north (or geographic north, i.e., the location of the geographic north pole). He further reasoned that as oxygen made up a significant proportion of the earth's atmosphere, variations in air temperature (and therefore the magnetic strength of oxygen) must be a major contributor to magnetic variation.

He began to analyze data from a number of magnetic observatories which had been established across the

British Empire, such as Toronto, Greenwich, Hobart, and Singapore. Faraday then produced his findings using graphical representations of the data to prove that there existed a correlation. His findings were later found to be incorrect, but the episode serves to demonstrate Faraday's habit of taking experimental results and expanding them over a whole world scenario.

Despite its lack of success, Faraday's experiments into atmospheric magnetism were just one part of a broader campaign, to prove his magnetic field theory and his lines of force theory. The latter was theorized as an alternative to established theory that vibrating atoms were the source of energy in the universe. Faraday rejected this, claiming instead that lines of force were the fundamental building blocks of space and matter. Where these lines intersected so matter was created. His work in mapping electrical force onto his Faraday Cage and establishing the magnetic force present in all matter and gas were all part of these theories.

A problem for any new theory proposed by Faraday on the fundamental nature of space, force, and matter was that he was operating in a highly qualitative state. He had no mathematical proof of this assertions, whereas the established order he was seeking to topple, did. This began to change as Faraday became involved in the project to extend telegraph cables across the Atlantic. The technical problem which the Atlantic, or indeed any long-distance telegraph, suffered was that signals became unintelligible the longer the lines were.

Faraday examined the problem, and his friend William Thomson set about creating a mathematical model which described the state of the electrical charge at the end of the cable. Armed with a mathematical proof of his theory, Faraday attended a meeting at the Institution of Civil Engineering in 1857. He claimed that a signal could be passed through the cable once every two seconds. This was sufficient for the corporate underwriters of the project to proceed. As Faraday himself had once said, as a good experimentalist, he had found a useful application for his theory.

The mathematization of Faraday's theories on the electrical telegraph model suggested that more of his theories could similarly be proven by mathematics. The man who would do this with Faraday's lines of force theory was James Clerk Maxwell. Maxwell was a graduate of Oxford who had been recommended to look at Faraday's experiments by William Thomson. Maxwell devoted himself to mathematization of Faraday's work and read his paper to the Cambridge Philosophical Society in December 1855 and February 1856. It was published later in 1856, and Faraday read the paper in early 1857.

Finally, Faraday's theories had received a mathematical proof. They had become quantifiable and not merely his own qualitative interpretations of the results of his experiments. In 1865, Maxwell produced another paper called *A Dynamical Theory of the Electromagnetic Field*. This paper provided a mathematical validation of Faraday's earlier hypothesis on the nature of light and electromagnetism. Maxwell confirmed Faraday's theories that electric and magnetic fields move through space as waves and that light is a undulation in the same field. Essentially, Maxwell proved Faraday's long-held belief of a unified field linking light, electrical force, and magnetism.

It was this work, first purported by Faraday and proved by Maxwell that formed the foundation for the later discovery of radio waves. It is difficult to imagine the twentieth century without radio waves and all the developments that followed. Faraday's theory made the discovery of radio waves possible, and Maxwell's mathematical proof made Faraday's theory widely known and accepted.

Chapter Seven

Famous Faraday

"Nature is our kindest friend and best critic in experimental science if we only allow her intimations to fall unbiased upon our minds."

—Michael Faraday

After initially refusing to have his famous Christmas Lectures published, Faraday eventually allowed William Crookes to release some of his lectures in book form. The result was *The Chemical History of a Candle* which was published in 1861. This book has since gone on to achieve great success, having never been out of print and translated into numerous languages such as French, Polish, and Japanese. Faraday was lauded by those who attended his lectures. Many celebrities of the day attended, and there is evidence that they were regarded as popular entertainment. Faraday had an easy way of talking to his audience that persuaded them that they understood the subject on which he was speaking.

One other reason for Faraday's popularity was his awareness of the social value of science. He was not a scientist in his ivory tower, making discoveries for the sake of discovery and with no other goal than the expansion of knowledge. He was an experimentalist, first and foremost, and believed that his role was to show the value of science to society. This was a major contributory factor to the popularity of science within the Victorian era. By the 1850s, as a result of his publications, his lectures, and his work as a scientific advisor to successive governments, Faraday's opinions were impossible to ignore and frequently sought.

Faraday had been invited to give an opinion on the phenomenon of mesmerism in the 1830s and had chosen to keep his counsel. This had been a fad at the time whereby mesmerists could heal ailments by passing magnets over the body. Because of the link to universal magnetism, Faraday appears to have been interested in the subject briefly, attending demonstrations by John Elliotson at University College and accepting an invitation from Isambard Brunel to a further demonstration. While privately he came to reject mesmerism, Faraday never publicly gave his views. By the 1850s, however, he appears to have become more confident in making known his views on controversial subjects.

An example of this is the phenomenon of table-turning which appeared in London in 1853. During seances, tables were being seen to levitate, turn, and even fly out of windows. Because it was believed there was some connection to electromagnetism, Faraday's opinions were requested. He attended two seances in June 1853 and concluded that the phenomenon was merely the result of involuntary and entirely unconscious muscular twitches of the participants involved. He published his views in the journal the *Athenaeum* and in a letter to *The Times*.

Faraday expressed the view that the popular belief in the phenomenon of table-turning was more a demonstration of the state of public education than anything of a scientific nature.

Faraday's views on education led to a series of lectures being created by the Royal Institution, entitled Lectures on Education. Faraday delivered the second of these lectures on May 6, 1854, chaired by Prince Albert (husband and Prince Consort to Queen Victoria). In contrast to his previous lectures, Faraday wrote out the lecture in its entirety. He wanted them to be read and critiqued as widely as possible. This represents a significant change from views of 20 years before. It demonstrates the confidence which Faraday possessed, both in his knowledge and its potential benefit to the wider public.

On July 7, 1855, following a steamboat trip on the Thames, Faraday was so disgusted by the amount of pollution that he wrote to *The Times* to warn of the potential risks. He knew that his opinions would be published by one of the foremost newspapers in the country and that they would subsequently be read and taken seriously. In the 30 years from the 1830s to the 1860s, Faraday's advice was sought on a wide range of topics, and he appears to have given his time willingly to each request. There is some evidence, however, that he disliked certain tasks and regarded them as a waste of his time. The glass experiments he took on during his time as assistant to Sir Humphry Davy are a prime example of that. In these cases, Faraday's resentment seems to stem primarily from taking on a task for which any number of other scientists existed to help.

Faraday had helped to popularize science, and the numbers pursuing it as a profession had increased significantly during his 30 years of professional success. Not only were Faraday's thoughts and words famous, but his face was too. Faraday had been an early patron of William Henry Talbot Fox in 1839, for his invention of a photographic process. Faraday was fascinated by this process for the rest of his life and posed for many photographs. He was depicted in portraiture frequently, one of the most painted men of his age. His portrait was captured by some of the leading portraitists of the era. These images were then reproduced as prints to feed a hungry market for celebrity images that would be familiar to our modern era.

Faraday was also an avid collector of prints of famous people, maintaining an album in which he would show the image and, on a facing page, a letter written to him by the person portrayed. This serves to illustrate his fame and the esteem with which he was held. The blacksmith's son was by the 1850s moving within a circle of celebrity.

Faraday was not just a household name; he had lifted himself out of the poverty of his origins. He could now count royalty among his close friends. After meeting Faraday, Prince Albert regularly chaired lectures at the Royal Institution. In 1855 he brought his two sons to see Faraday's Christmas Lecture. He then offered a house on the Hampton Court Estate to Faraday and his family. They moved into the house in September 1858. Faraday spent part of the year there and took permanent residence in 1866. Michael Faraday would spend his last days on the estate, dying there on August 27, 1866, one month before his 76th birthday. He was survived by his devoted wife Sarah.

Conclusion

Following the death of Michael Faraday, a public subscription was started for a statue of him. It would depict Faraday holding an induction ring. This demonstrates what was, in the public imagination, the major breakthrough of Michael Faraday's career. It speaks to his success and subsequent fame that an electromagnet and the concept of electromagnetic induction would be considered for such a publicly funded memorial. After all, much of the public would not necessarily understand the electromagnetic field theory which Faraday postulated, nor would they have the benefit of a modern hindsight, including a full view of the technology and innovation which followed Faraday's discoveries. The statue remains at the entrance of the Royal Institution following its unveiling in 1876.

Faraday created a spark which went on to become a pivotal driving force of the twentieth and twenty-first centuries. Without his discoveries, our era would most likely be unrecognizable. Faraday gave scientific plausibility to the burgeoning electrical industry. This industry was in direct competition with the steam locomotive and gas lighting industries, both of which were financially and politically entrenched. The electrical industrial complex recognized this by naming the unit by which capacitance was measured a farad. And the first custom-made telegraph cable laying ship was named the *Faraday*.

In 1931, Faraday's discovery of induction was commemorated with an Electrical Exhibition in the Queen's Hall. This included displays of Faraday's equipment as well as the various pieces of modern technology made possible by his discovery. This was one hundred years from Faraday's publication of his findings on induction, and the subject was considered of such importance in the intervening century that ten thousand pounds were spent in putting on the exhibition. Prime Minister Ramsay MacDonald said in his opening address (which was broadcast on radio) that his address would not have been possible but for Faraday's work. This is a telling statement and evidence of the impact Faraday had on his time and the future direction of the human race. Radio, television, electrical power, each with its own offshoots of technological developments and sciences, but all come from the same small group of theories and the same mind.

Michael Faraday was self-educated but elevated his mind to the pinnacle of human thought. He re-imagined his world, seeing it in a new way and making connections which few had made before. He then set about trying to prove his theories correct. He lived in a time when social class was an almost unbreakable straight jacket. Not only was it difficult to transcend the class of your origins but many believed that it should not be done. Yet Faraday, through his intellect, was able to do just that. He began his life in a poor area of London as the son of a blacksmith. His notebooks were enough to see him employed at the Royal Institution and his work there to see him made a

Fellow of the Royal Society and become a man whose views were respected at the highest levels of society.

His life continues to be celebrated. In the 1980s the Faraday Award was founded and given to the practicing scientist who had made the most significant contribution to public awareness and understanding of science. In 1991 Michael Faraday replaced William Shakespeare on the 20-pound note in commemoration of his bicentennial. His book *Experimental Researches* has been called one of the books that changed the world. In 2006 a project to refurbish state school laboratories was dubbed Project Faraday.

Despite his fame and the impact of his discoveries, Faraday was a modest man. He remained until his death a devout member of the Sandemanian church and happily married to his wife, Sarah. None of his fame appears to have changed him. A man of his vision must have been aware of how far-reaching his discoveries would be, but despite this success, he was clearly a man who held his religious beliefs dear. His storming out of a meeting with Lord Melbourne after the prime minister had uttered profanities demonstrates how seriously he took his faith. He was an Elder in the Sandemanian church, taking on the role at a point in his life when he could ill afford any time from his work. By holding true to his beliefs, he placed himself out of step with mainstream, Anglican society. And yet he didn't waver. Such was his character and brilliance that Michael Faraday was accepted, even by those at the head of the very establishments which he rejected.

Made in the USA
Lexington, KY
03 March 2019